Copyright © 2014 Hallmark Licensing, LLC

Published by Hallmark Gift Books,
a division of Hallmark Cards, Inc.,
Kansas City, MO 64141
Visit us on the Web at Hallmark.com.

All rights reserved. No part of this publication may be reproduced,
transmitted, or stored in any form or by any means without the prior
written permission of the publisher.

Editorial Director: Delia Berrigan
Editor: Kim Schworm Acosta
Art Director: Jan Mastin
Designer: Mary Eakin
Production Designer: Dan Horton

ISBN: 978-1-59530-862-7
BOK2157

Printed and bound in China
NOV14

Being a Grandma's a Marvelous Thing!

By Linda Barnes

Hallmark

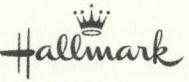

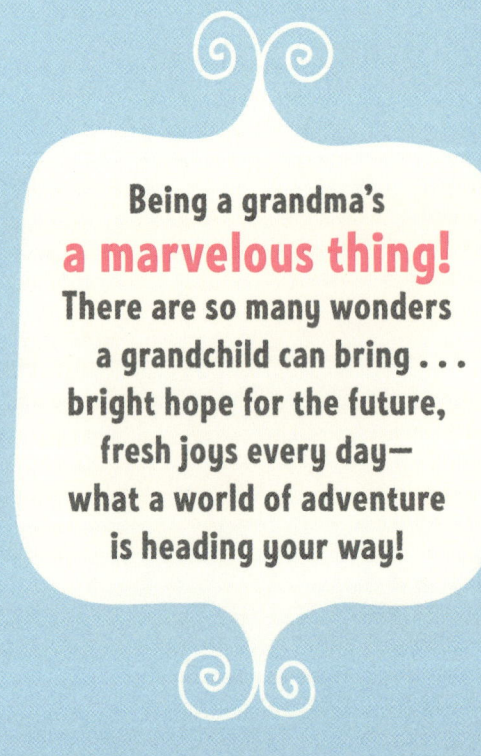

Being a grandma's
a marvelous thing!
There are so many wonders
a grandchild can bring . . .
bright hope for the future,
fresh joys every day—
what a world of adventure
is heading your way!

This child of your child means a new generation

of loving and laughing and **great celebration.**

Your family is starting to write a **new chapter,**

with more happy stories to add ever after!

The role of a grandma
may take getting used to.
It isn't a thing
you just do if you choose to.

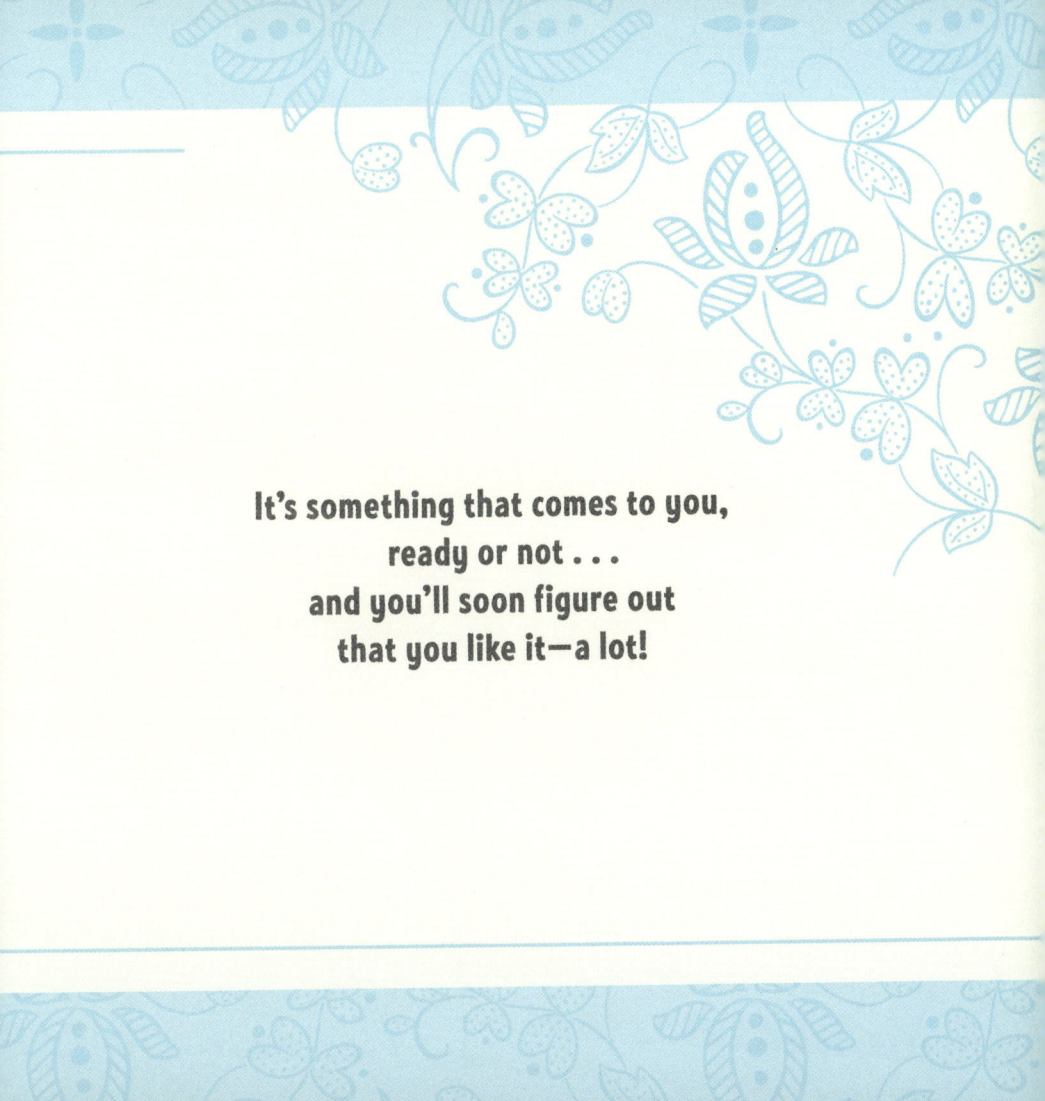

It's something that comes to you,
ready or not . . .
and you'll soon figure out
that you like it—a lot!

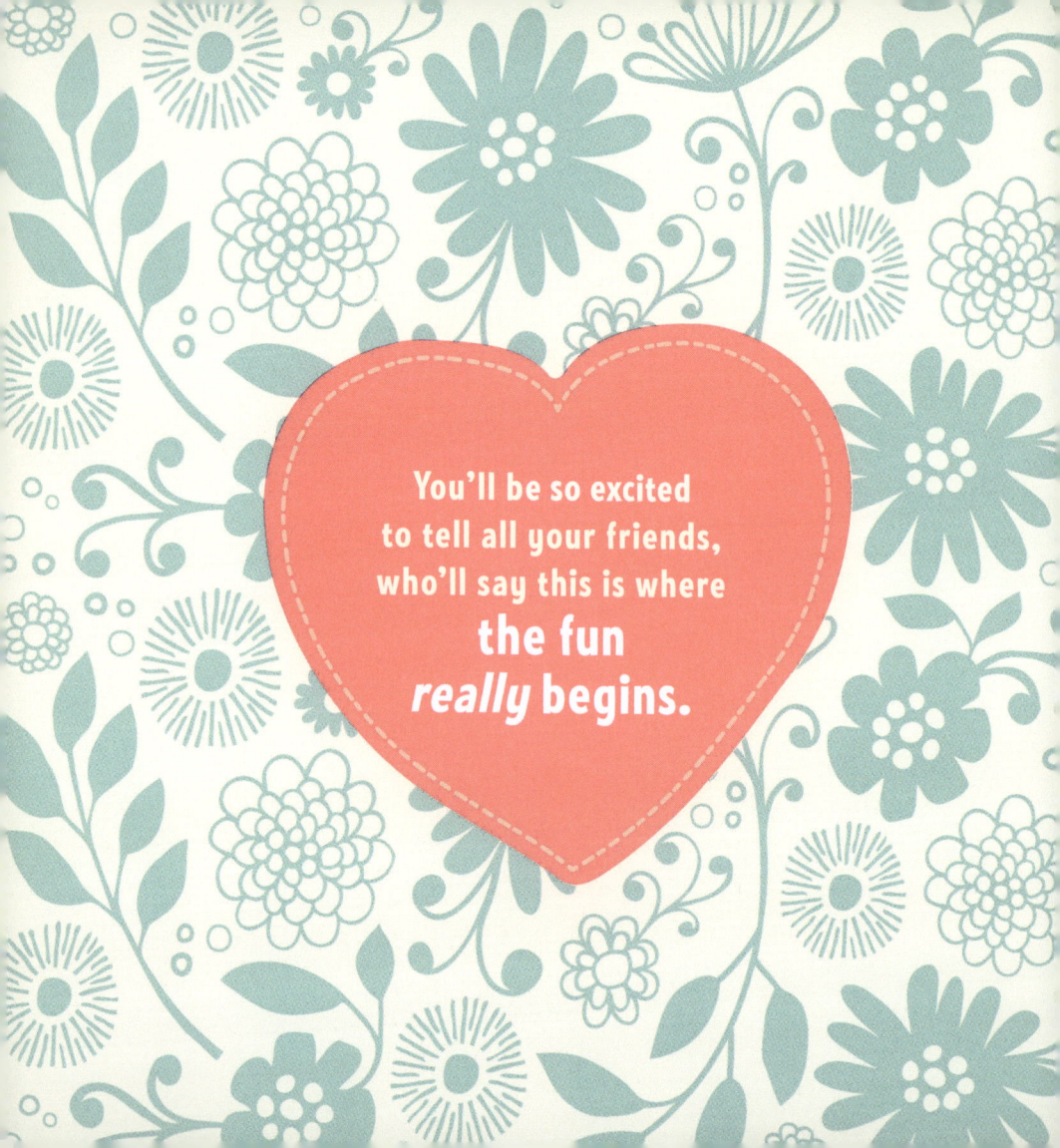

There are cool toys to find,
tiny outfits to buy,
and adorable furniture,
"only this high!"

Then the
big day
arrives,

and the first time you meet,
you're convinced that you've
never known
someone so sweet.

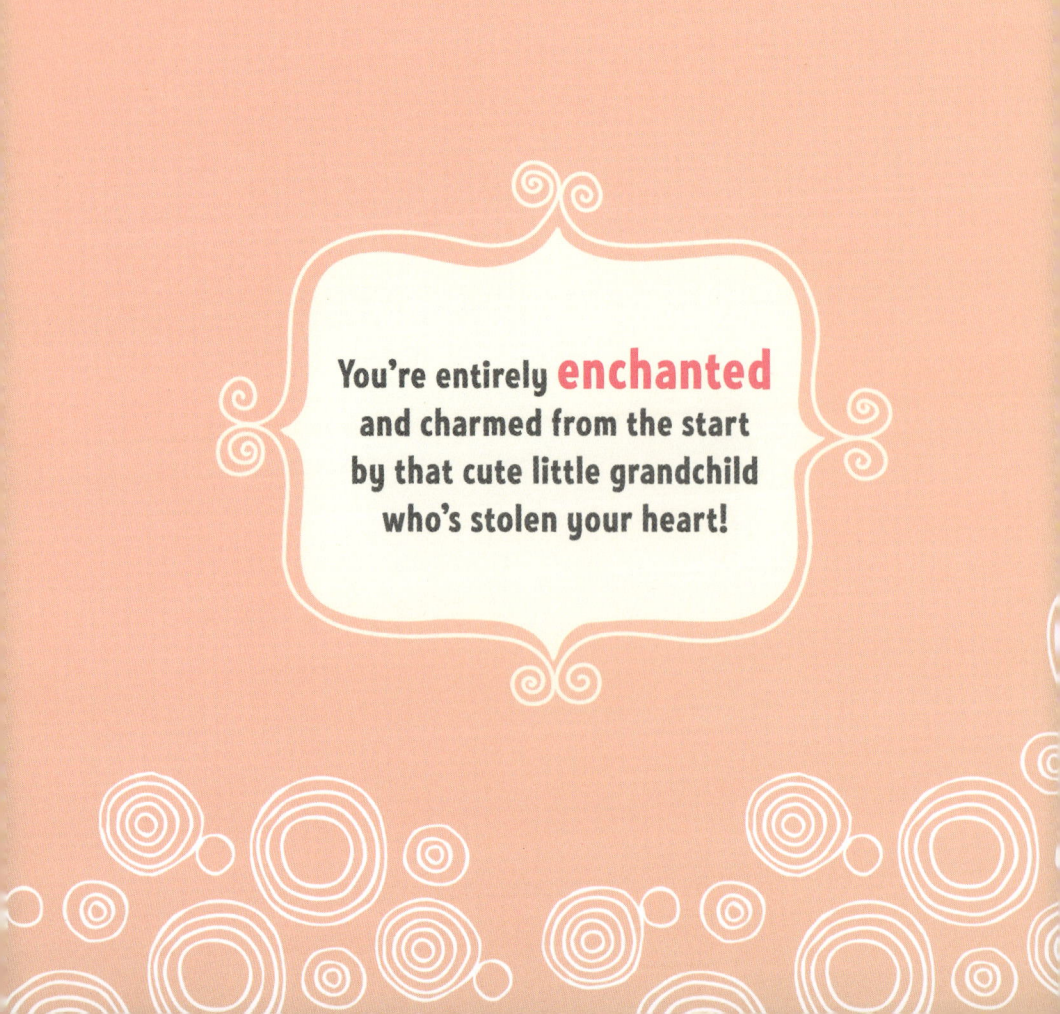

You're entirely **enchanted** and charmed from the start by that cute little grandchild who's stolen your heart!

There are
miracle moments
and simple delights,
days of discovery
and lullaby nights . . .
plump little fingers . . .
kissable toes . . .

**and love so amazing
your heart overflows!**

And the pictures!

They'll take on
a life of their own
as you fill up your camera,
your albums, your phone!
You'll be showing them off
to friends, family, and more—
even grandmas behind you
in line at the store!

A grandchild brings plenty of reasons to smile,

plus the chance to discover your own grandma style.

You can color,
tell stories,
play dress-up, or sing—

because grandmas can do just about **anything!**

A plan guaranteed to make everyone's day begins with,
"Can Grandma come over to play?"

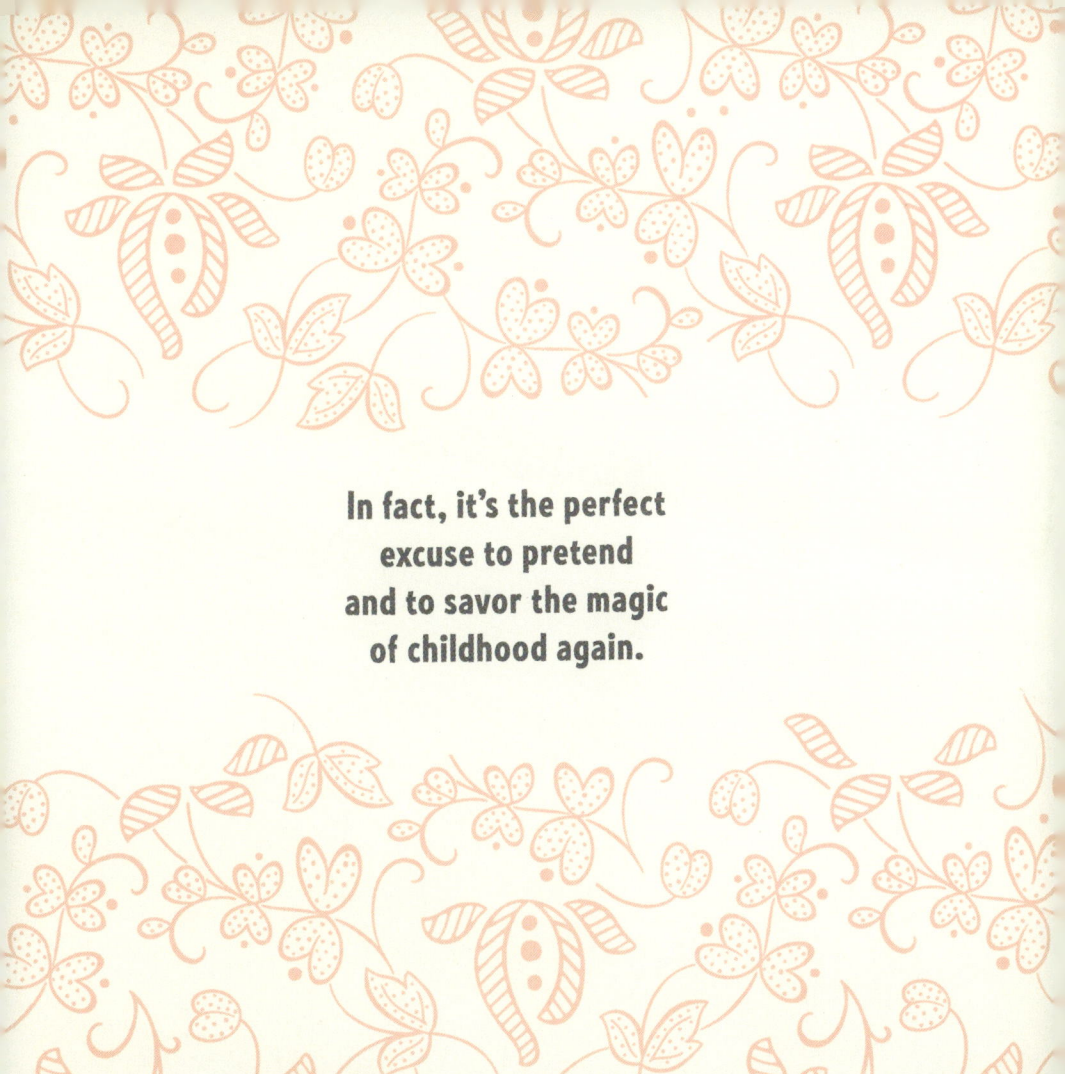

In fact, it's the perfect
excuse to pretend
and to savor the magic
of childhood again.

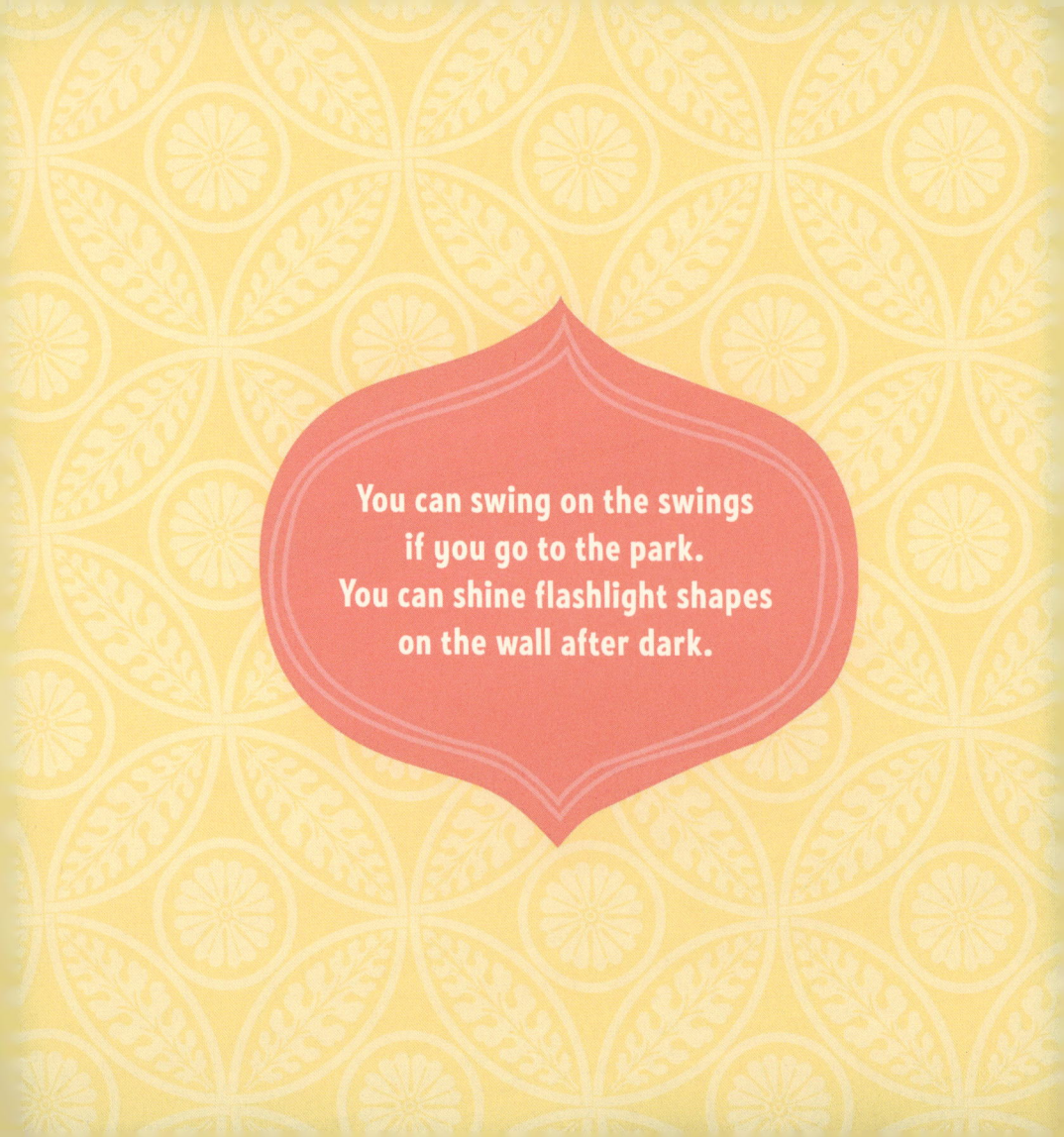

You can swing on the swings
if you go to the park.
You can shine flashlight shapes
on the wall after dark.

**You can fly paper airplanes,
make dandelion wishes,
or cast in rain puddles
for make-believe fishes!**

A true guilty pleasure
most grandmas confess to

is all the requests
that you get to say **"yes"** to.

**"Yes" to more cookies!
"Yes" to balloons!**

"Yes" to late bedtimes
and **extra cartoons!**

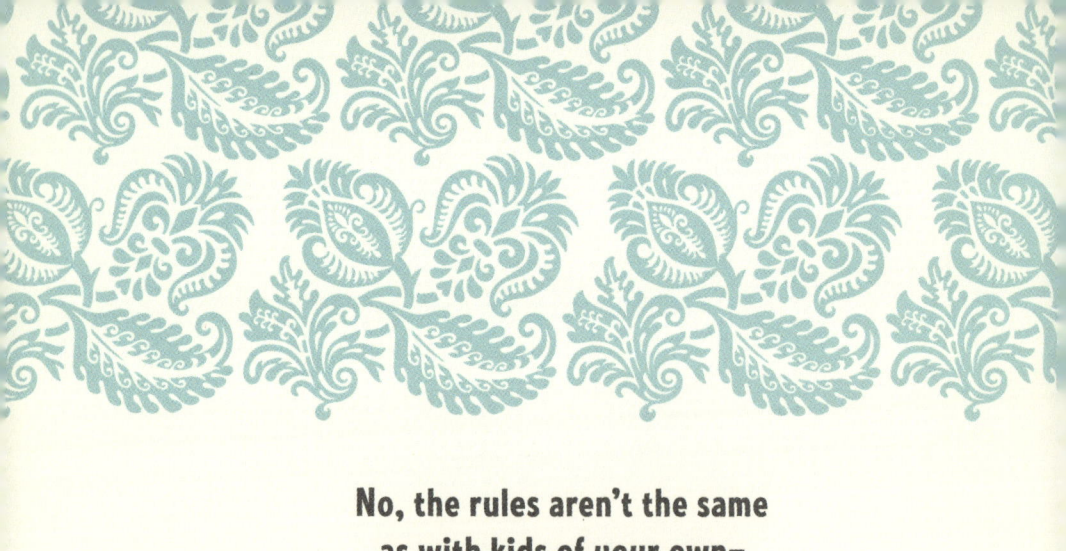

No, the rules aren't the same
as with kids of your own—
you just love 'em and spoil 'em
and send 'em back home!

Then, you gladly sit down
for some much-needed rest
so you'll be in top form
for your next **grandkid-fest!**

You'll think that your grandchild is smarter than smart!

Your fridge will be covered with awesome kid art.

You'll recognize french fries as **first-class cuisine,**

and you'll always have change
for the gumball machine!

Kids love **Grandma's kitchen,**
where messes don't matter
and nobody cares
if you eat half the batter!

Stir in a few sprinkles
of joy and delight,
and the memories you're making
will turn out just right.

You'll give your grandkids
your total attention,
someone to admire
their most recent invention,

unlimited smiles,
lots of hugs and high fives,
and a **love that goes with them**
the rest of their lives!

And their **gifts to YOU**
will be moments to treasure,
together times, laughter,
and love beyond measure—

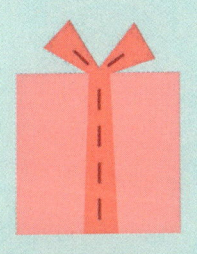

rewards that remind you
how richly you're blessed
because being a grandma
is simply . . .

THE BEST!

If you have enjoyed this book
or it has touched your life in some way,
we would love to hear from you.

Please send your comments to:
Hallmark Book Feedback
P.O. Box 419034
Mail Drop 100
Kansas City, MO 64141

Or e-mail us at:
booknotes@hallmark.com